THE *Best*
IN MOVIE SHEET MUSIC

STAR WARS TRILOGY SPECIAL EDITION LOGO: ®, TM AND © 1997 Lucasfilm Ltd

Project Manager: Carol Cuellar
Cover Design: Frank Milone & Debbie Lipton

© 1997 WARNER BROS. PUBLICATIONS
All Rights Reserved

CONTENTS

AFTER ALL
(Love Theme from "Chances Are")

Words and Music by
DEAN PITCHFORD and
TOM SNOW

After All - 5 - 1

4

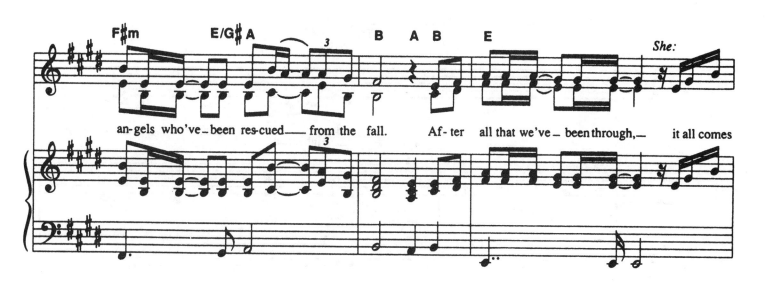

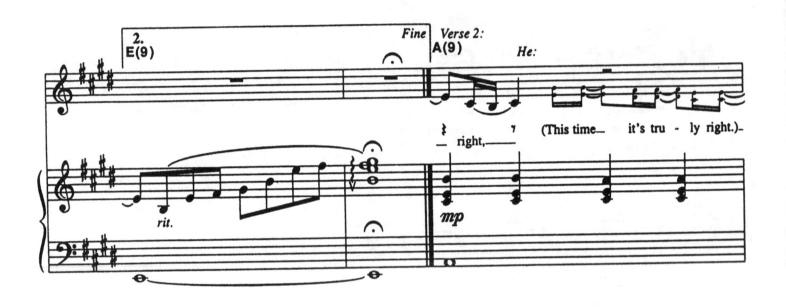

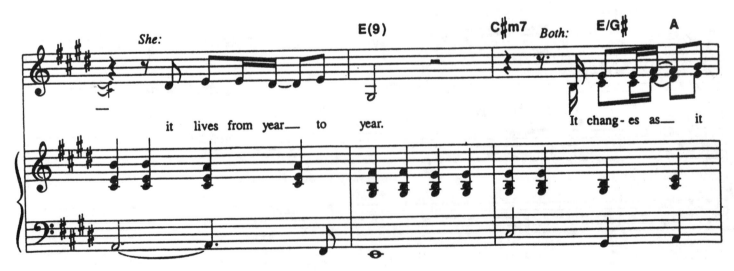

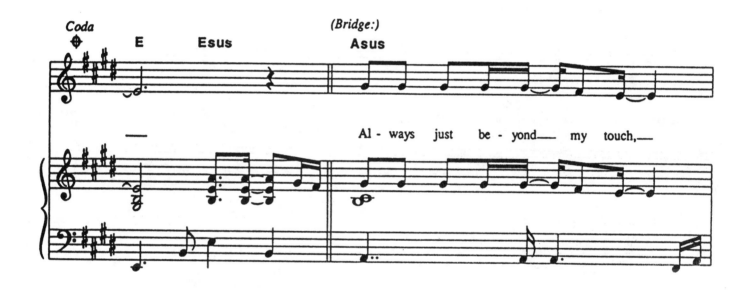

After All - 5 - 5

From Walt Disney's "BEAUTY AND THE BEAST"

BEAUTY AND THE BEAST

Lyrics by
HOWARD ASHMAN

Music by
ALAN MENKEN

10

13

Beauty and the Beast - 6 - 6

BECAUSE YOU LOVED ME
(Theme from "Up Close & Personal")

Words and Music by
DIANE WARREN

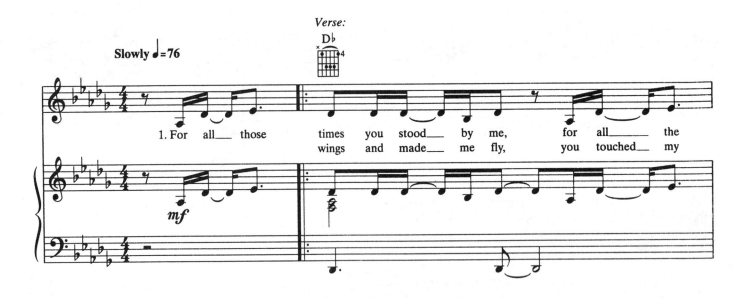

Verse:

Slowly ♩=76

1. For all___ those times you stood___ by me, for all___ the
wings and made___ me fly, you touched___ my

truth that you made me see, for all___ the joy you brought to my life,___ for all___ the
hand, I could touch the sky. I lost___ my faith you gave it back to me. You said___ no

wrong that you___ made right, for ev - ery___ dream you made___ come true, for all___ the
star was out___ of reach, you stood___ by___ me and I_____ stood tall. I had___ your

Because You Loved Me - 5 - 1

16

FOR YOU I WILL

Words and Music by
DIANE WARREN

20

For You I Will - 5 - 2

For You I Will - 5 - 3

22

For You I Will - 5 - 4

CAN YOU FEEL THE LOVE TONIGHT

Lyrics by
TIM RICE

Music by
ELTON JOHN

COUNT ON ME

Words and Music by
BABYFACE, WHITNEY HOUSTON
and MICHAEL HOUSTON

Count on Me - 6 - 1

From the Twentieth Century-Fox Motion Picture "ONE FINE DAY"

FOR THE FIRST TIME

Words and Music by
JAMES NEWTON HOWARD,
ALLAN RICH and JUD FRIEDMAN

Slowly ♩ = 62

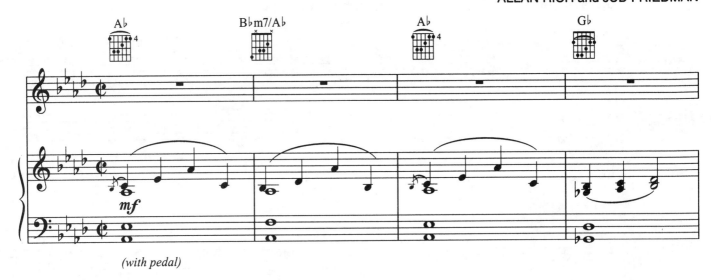

(with pedal)

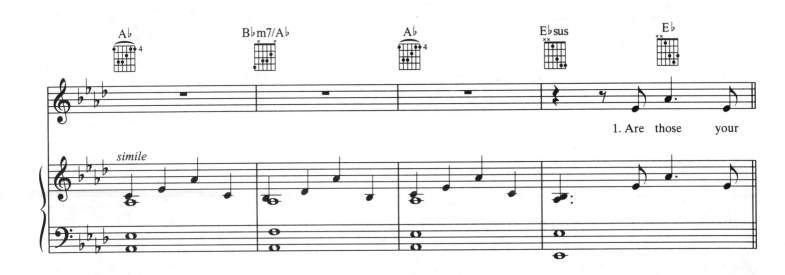

1. Are those your

Verse:

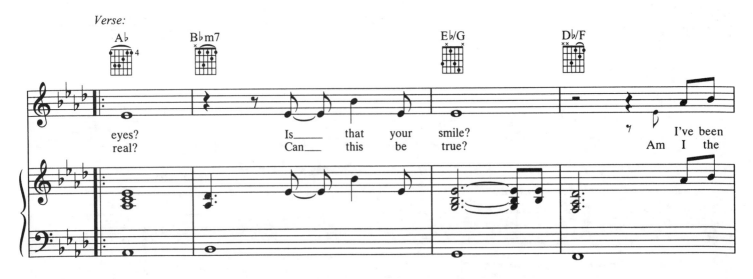

eyes? Is___ that your smile? I've been
real? Can___ this be true? Am I the

For the First Time - 6 - 1

A♭
D♭
E♭sus
E♭
first time, I'm seeing who you are. I can't believe
D♭/F
D♭m/F♭
A♭/E♭
D♭
D♭m6
how much I see when you're looking back at me. Now I
A♭/E♭
Fm7
B♭m7
E♭sus
E♭
understand what love is, love is for the
A♭
Fm7
D♭maj9
1.
E♭sus
E♭
first time. 2. Can this be

I BELIEVE I CAN FLY

Words and Music by
R. KELLY

42

I Believe I Can Fly - 5 - 3

43

I Believe I Can Fly - 5 - 4

44

I Believe I Can Fly - 5 - 5

I JUST CALLED TO SAY I LOVE YOU

Moderately ♩ = 112

Words and Music by
STEVIE WONDER

I Just Called to Say I Love You - 5 - 1

I Just Called to Say I Love You - 5 - 3

48

I Just Called to Say I Love You - 5 - 4

Verse 3:

No summer's high; no warm July;
No harvest moon to light one tender August night.
No autumn breeze; no falling leaves;
Not even time for birds to fly to southern skies.

Verse 4:

No Libra sun; no Halloween;
No giving thanks to all the Christmas joy you bring.
But what it is, though old so new
To fill your heart like no three words could ever do.

(To Chorus:)

From the Motion Picture "THE PREACHER'S WIFE"

I BELIEVE IN YOU AND ME

Words and Music by
SANDY LINZER and DAVID WOLFERT

53

Verse 2:
I will never leave your side,
I will never hurt your pride.
When all the chips are down,
I will always be around,
Just to be right where you are, my love.
Oh, I love you, boy.
I will never leave you out,
I will always let you in
To places no one has ever been.
Deep inside, can't you see?
I believe in you and me.
(To Bridge:)

I Believe in You and Me - 4 - 4

From the Motion Picture "THE MIRROR HAS TWO FACES"

I FINALLY FOUND SOMEONE

Words and Music by
BARBRA STREISAND, MARVIN HAMLISCH,
R.J. LANGE and BRYAN ADAMS

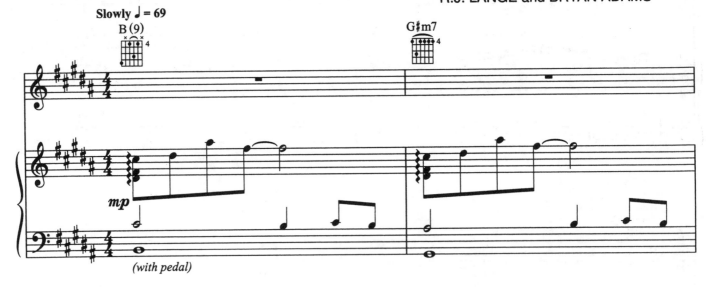

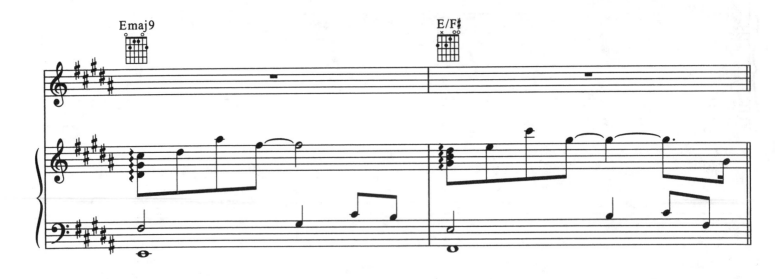

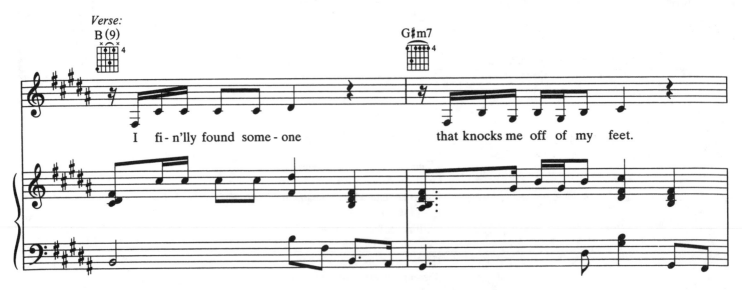

I Finally Found Someone - 8 - 1

I Finally Found Someone - 8 - 2

56

I Finally Found Someone - 8 - 8

KISSING YOU
(Love Theme From "ROMEO + JULIET")

Words and Music by
DES'REE and TIM ATACK

Chorus:

ev - er._____ 'Cause I'm_____ kiss - ing you,_____ oh._____

I'm_____ kiss - ing you._____

From the Original Motion Picture Soundtrack "8 SECONDS"

LANE'S THEME

Composed by
BILL CONTI

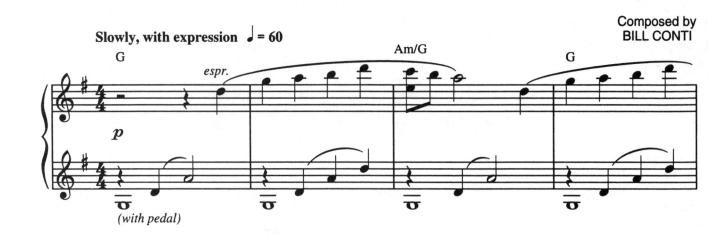

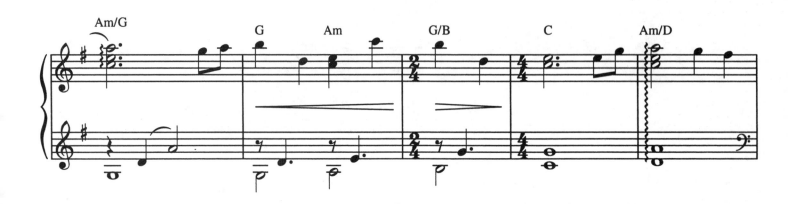

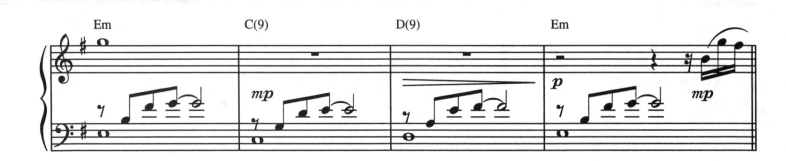

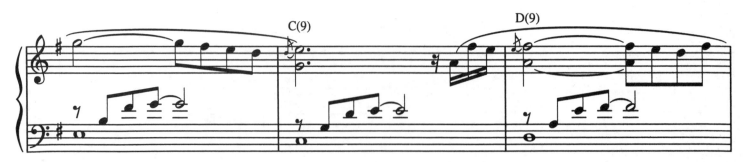

Lane's Theme - 4 - 1

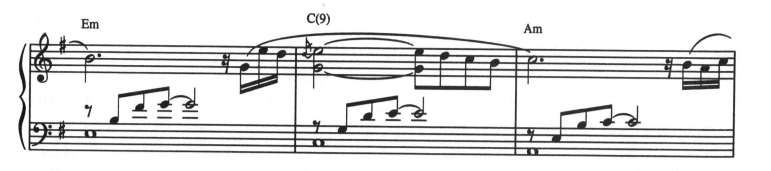

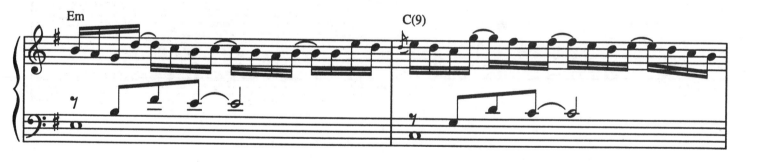

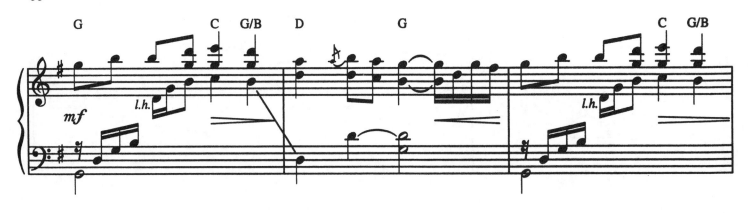

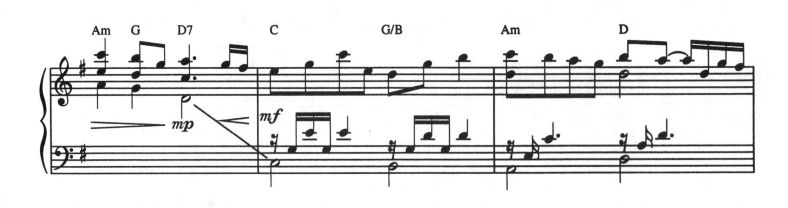

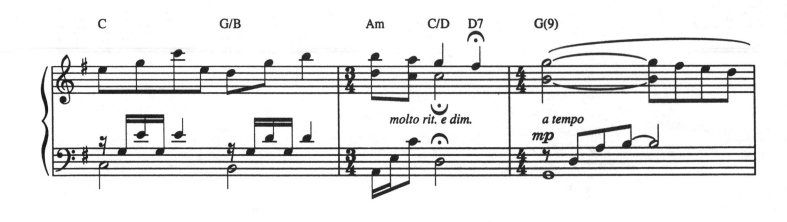

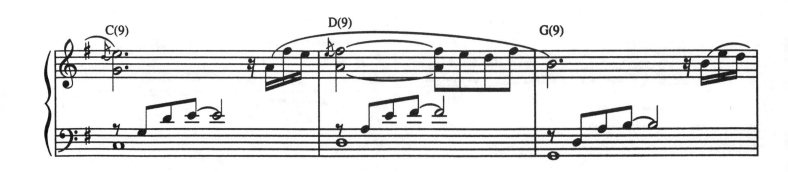

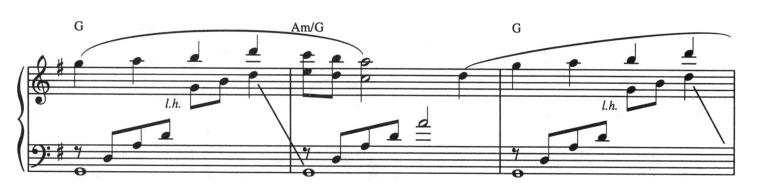

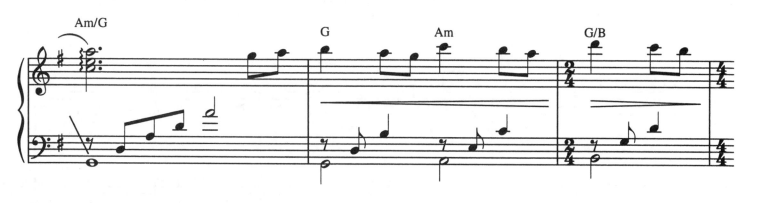

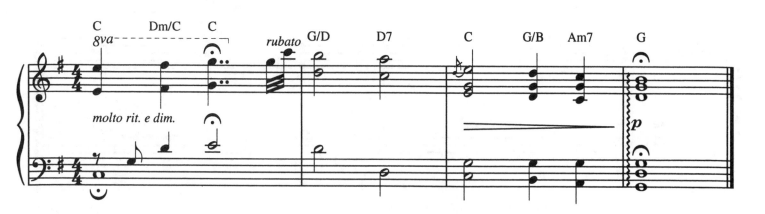

Lane's Theme - 4 - 4

From the TV Show "PEANUTS SPECIAL"
LINUS AND LUCY

By
VINCE GUARALDI

Linus and Lucy - 2 - 1

Linus and Lucy - 2 - 2

8va bassa

THE PINK PANTHER

Music by
HENRY MANCINI

The Pink Panther - 2 - 1

The Pink Panther - 2 - 2

SEND IN THE CLOWNS

Music and Lyrics by
STEPHEN SONDHEIM

Send in the Clowns - 3 - 1

Send in the Clowns - 3 - 2

From the Columbia Pictures Release "YOU LIGHT UP MY LIFE"

YOU LIGHT UP MY LIFE

Words and Music by
JOE BROOKS

78

*From the Lucasfilm Ltd. Productions "STAR WARS", "THE EMPIRE STRIKES BACK"
and "RETURN OF THE JEDI" - Twentieth Century-Fox Releases.*

STAR WARS
(Main Theme)

Music by
JOHN WILLIAMS

Star Wars - 2 - 1

Star Wars - 2 - 2

THAT'S WHAT FRIENDS ARE FOR

Words and Music by
CAROLE BAYER SAGER and
BURT BACHARACH

That's What Friends Are for - 3 - 1

84

From "GONE WITH THE WIND"

TARA THEME

Music by
MAX STEINER

From the Vestron Motion Picture "DIRTY DANCING"

(I'VE HAD) THE TIME OF MY LIFE

Words and Music by
FRANKE PREVITE, DONALD MARKOWITZ
and JOHN DeNICOLA

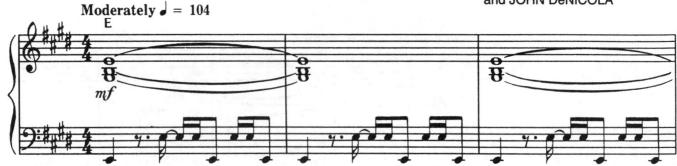

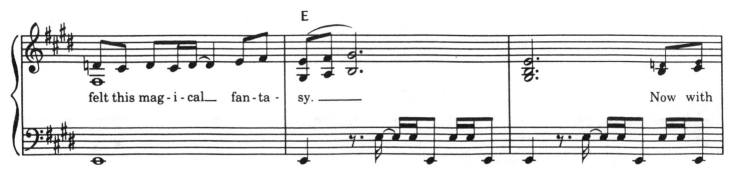

(I've Had) The Time of My Life - 4 - 1

88

Verse 2:
With my body and soul
I want you more than you'll ever know.
So we'll just let it go,
Don't be afraid to lose control.
Yes, I know what's on your mind
When you say, "Stay with me tonight."
Just remember . . .

(I've Had) The Time of My Life - 4 - 4

From the Broadway Musical "ANNIE"

TOMORROW

Lyric by
MARTIN CHARNIN

Music by
CHARLES STROUSE

(small notes are optional harmony)

92

SINGIN' IN THE RAIN

Lyrics by
ARTHUR FREED

Music by
NACIO HERB BROWN

Singin' in the Rain - 5 - 1

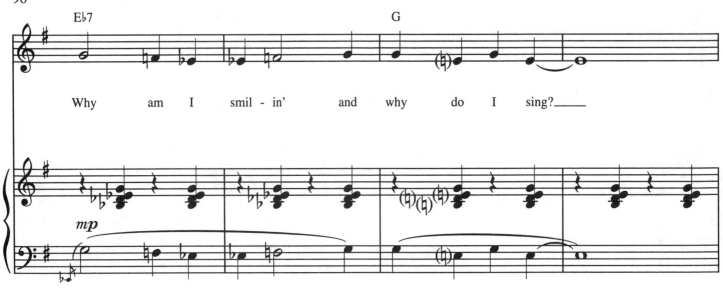

Why am I smil - in' and why do I sing?____

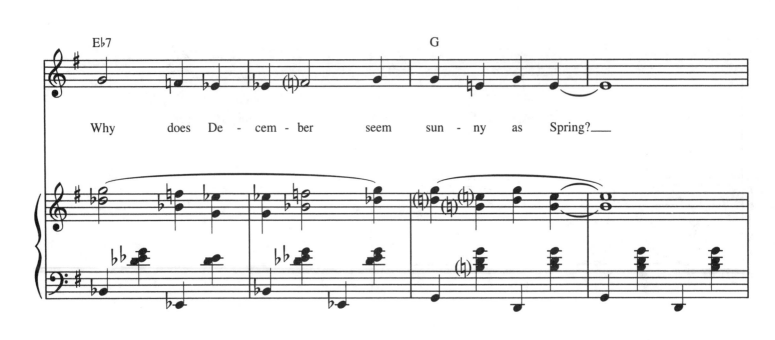

Why does De - cem - ber seem sun - ny as Spring?____

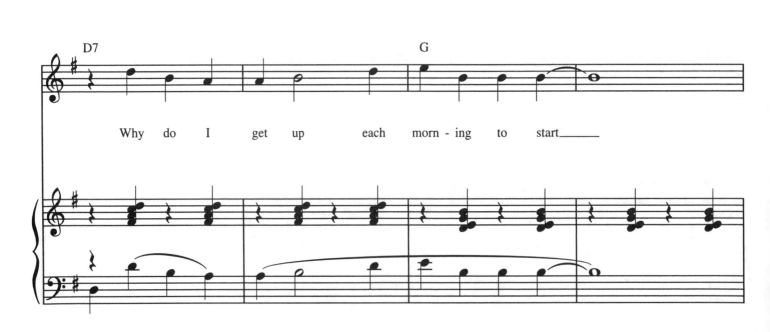

Why do I get up each morn - ing to start____

Showstoppers

100 or more titles in each volume of this Best-Selling Series!

Piano/Vocal/Chords:

20's, 30's, & 40's SHOWSTOPPERS
(F2865SMX)

100 nostalgic favorites include: Chattanooga Choo Choo • Pennsylvania 6-5000 • Blue Moon • Moonglow • My Blue Heaven • Ain't Misbehavin' • That Old Black Magic and more.

50's & 60's SHOWSTOPPERS
(F2864SMB)

Bop back to a simpler time and enjoy: Aquarius/Let the Sunshine In • (Sittin' On) The Dock of the Bay • Hey, Good Lookin' • Sunny • Johnny Angel and more.

70's & 80's SHOWSTOPPERS
P/V/C (F2863SME)
Easy Piano (F2863P2X)

100 pop songs from two decades. Titles include: Anything for You • Blue Bayou • Hungry Eyes • I Wanna Dance with Somebody (Who Loves Me) • If You Say My Eyes Are Beautiful • I'll Never Love This Way Again • Isn't She Lovely • Old Time Rock & Roll • When the Night Comes.

BIG NOTE PIANO SHOWSTOPPERS
Vol. 1 (F2871P3C)   Vol. 2 (F2918P3A)

Easy-to-read big note arrangements of 100 popular tunes include: Do You Want to Know a Secret? • If Ever You're in My Arms Again • Moon River • Over the Rainbow • Singin' in the Rain • You Light Up My Life • Theme from *Love Story*.

BROADWAY SHOWSTOPPERS
(F2878SMB)

100 great show tunes include: Ain't Misbehavin' • Almost Like Being in Love • Consider Yourself • Give My Regards to Broadway • Good Morning Starshine • Mood Indigo • Send in the Clowns • Tomorrow.

CHRISTMAS SHOWSTOPPERS
P/V/C (F2868SMA)
Easy Piano (F2924P2X)
Big Note (F2925P3X)

100 favorite holiday songs including: Sleigh Ride • Silver Bells • Deck the Halls • Have Yourself a Merry Little Christmas • Here Comes Santa Claus • Little Drummer Boy • Let It Snow! Let It Snow! Let It Snow!

CLASSICAL PIANO SHOWSTOPPERS
(F2872P9X)

100 classical intermediate piano solos include: Arioso • Bridal Chorus (from *Lohengrin*) • Clair de Lune • Fifth Symphony (Theme) • Minuet in G • Moonlight Sonata (1st Movement) • Polovetsian Dance (from *Prince Igor*) • The Swan • Wedding March (from *A Midsummer Night's Dream*).

COUNTRY SHOWSTOPPERS
(F2902SMC)

A fine collection of 101 favorite country classics and standards including: Cold, Cold Heart • For the Good Times • I'm So Lonesome I Could Cry • There's a Tear in My Beer • Young Country and more.

EASY GUITAR SHOWSTOPPERS
(F2934EGA)

100 guitar arrangements of new chart hits, old favorites, classics and solid gold songs. Includes melody, chords and lyrics for songs like: Didn't We • Love Theme from *St. Elmo's Fire* (For Just a Moment) • Out Here on My Own • Please Mr. Postman • Proud Mary • The Way He Makes Me Feel • With You I'm Born Again • You're the Inspiration.

EASY LISTENING SHOWSTOPPERS
(F3069SMX)

85 easy listening songs including popular favorites, standards, TV and movie selections like: After All (Love Theme from *Chances Are*) • From a Distance • The Greatest Love of All • Here We Are • Theme from *Ice Castles* (Through the Eyes of Love) • The Vows Go Unbroken (Always True to You) • You Are So Beautiful.

EASY ORGAN SHOWSTOPPERS
(F2873EOB)

100 great current hits and timeless standards in easy arrangements for organ include: After the Lovin' • Always and Forever • Come Saturday Morning • I Just Called to Say I Love You • Isn't She Lovely • On the Wings of Love • Up Where We Belong • You Light Up My Life.

EASY PIANO SHOWSTOPPERS
Vol. 1 (F2875P2D)   Vol. 2 (F2912P2C)

100 easy piano arrangements of familiar songs include: Alfie • Baby Elephant Walk • Classical Gas • Don't Cry Out Loud • Colour My World • The Pink Panther • I Honestly Love You.

JAZZ SHOWSTOPPERS
(F2953SMX)

101 standard jazz tunes including: Misty • Elmer's Tune • Birth of the Blues • It Don't Mean a Thing (If It Ain't Got That Swing).

MOVIE SHOWSTOPPERS
(F2866SMC)

100 songs from memorable motion pictures include: Axel F • Up Where We Belong • Speak Softly Love (from *The Godfather*) • The Entertainer • Fame • Nine to Five • Nobody Does It Better.

POPULAR PIANO SHOWSTOPPERS
(F2876P9B)

100 popular intermediate piano solos include: Baby Elephant Walk • Gonna Fly Now (Theme from *Rocky*) • The Hill Street Blues Theme • Love Is a Many-Splendored Thing • (Love Theme from) *Romeo and Juliet* • Separate Lives (Love Theme from *White Nights*) • The Shadow of Your Smile • Theme from *The Apartment* • Theme from *New York, New York*.

RAGTIME SHOWSTOPPERS
(F2867SMX)

These 100 original classic rags by Scott Joplin, James Scott, Joseph Lamb and other ragtime composers include: Maple Leaf Rag • The Entertainer • Kansas City Rag • Ma Rag Time Baby • The St. Louis Rag • World's Fair Rag and many others.

ROMANTIC SHOWSTOPPERS
(F2870SMC)

101 beautiful songs including: After All (Love Theme from *Chances Are*) • Here and Now • I Can't Stop Loving You • If You Say My Eyes Are Beautiful • The Vows Go Unbroken (Always True to You) • You Got It.

TELEVISION SHOWSTOPPERS
(F2874SMC)

103 TV themes including: Another World • Dear John • Hall or Nothing (The Arsenio Hall Show) • Star Trek -The Next Generation (Main Title) • Theme from "Cheers" (Where Everybody Knows Your Name).

The Book of *Golden* Series

**THE BOOK OF GOLDEN
ALL-TIME FAVORITES**
(F2939SMX) Piano/Vocal/Chords

**THE BOOK OF GOLDEN
BIG BAND FAVORITES**
(F3172SMX) Piano/Vocal/Chords

**THE BOOK OF GOLDEN
BROADWAY**
(F2986SMX) Piano/Vocal/Chords

**THE NEW BOOK OF GOLDEN
CHRISTMAS**
(F2478SMB) Piano/Vocal/Chords
(F2478EOX) Easy Organ
(F2478COX) Chord Organ

**THE BOOK OF GOLDEN
COUNTRY MUSIC**
(F2926SMA) Piano/Vocal/Chords

**THE BOOK OF GOLDEN
HAWAIIAN SONGS**
(F3113SMX) Piano/Vocal/Chords

**THE BOOK OF GOLDEN
IRISH SONGS**
(F3212SMX) Piano/Vocal/Chords

**THE BOOK OF GOLDEN
ITALIAN SONGS**
(F2907SMX) Piano/Vocal/Chords

THE BOOK OF GOLDEN JAZZ
(F3012SMX) Piano/Vocal/Chords

**THE NEW BOOK OF GOLDEN
LATIN SONGS**
(F3049SMX) Piano/Vocal/Chords

**THE NEW BOOK OF GOLDEN
LOVE SONGS**
(F2415SOX) Organ

**THE BOOK OF GOLDEN
MOTOWN SONGS**
(F3144SMX) Piano/Vocal/Chords

**THE NEW BOOK OF GOLDEN
MOVIE THEMES, Volume 1**
(F2810SMX) Piano/Vocal/Chords

**THE NEW BOOK OF GOLDEN
MOVIE THEMES, Volume 2**
(F2811SMX) Piano/Vocal/Chords

**THE BOOK OF GOLDEN
POPULAR FAVORITES**
(F2233SMX) Piano/Vocal/Chords

**THE BOOK OF GOLDEN
POPULAR PIANO SOLOS**
(F3193P9X) Intermediate/
Advanced Piano

**THE BOOK OF GOLDEN
ROCK 'N' ROLL**
(F2830SMB) Piano/Vocal/Chords

**THE NEW BOOK OF GOLDEN
WEDDING SONGS**
(F2265SMA) Piano/Vocal/Chords